I0197553

the Goddess Virgo

AND HER RELATIONSHIP WITH

CHRISTIANITY

A supernatural biography

by Peter Howe

the Goddess Virgo

AND HER RELATIONSHIP WITH

CHRISTIANITY

MEMOIRS

Cirencester

Published by Memoirs

MEMOIRS

Memoirs Books

25 Market Place, Cirencester, Gloucestershire, GL7 2NX

Tel: 01285 640485 Fax 01285 640487

info@memoirsbooks.co.uk www.memoirsbooks.co.uk

Copyright ©Peter Howe, May 2011

First published in England, May 2011

Book jacket design Ray Lipscombe

ISBN 978-1-908223-06-7

All rights reserved.

No part of this publication may be reproduced, stored in a retrieval system, or transmitted in any form or by any means, electronic, mechanical, photocopying, recording or otherwise without the prior permission of Memoirs.

Printed in England

The Thunder, Perfect Mind

From the Nag Hammadi Library, translated by George W. MacRae

The Nag Hammadi Library is a collection of ancient texts found by a peasant in 1945, buried in an earthenware jar near the town of Nag Hammadi in Upper Egypt. The manuscripts are thought to have been hidden by monks from a nearby monastery to preserve them from destruction. Some of the text is indecipherable.

I was sent forth from the power,

and I have come to those who reflect upon me,

and I have been found among those who seek after me.

Look upon me, you who reflect upon me,

and you hearers, hear me.

You who are waiting for me, take me to yourselves.

And do not banish me from your sight.

And do not make your voice hate me, nor your hearing.

Do not be ignorant of me anywhere or any time. Be on your guard!

Do not be ignorant of me.

For I am the first and the last.

I am the honoured one and the scorned one.

I am the whore and the holy one.

I am the wife and the virgin.

I am the mother and the daughter.

I am the members of my mother.

I am the barren one

and many are her sons.

I am she whose wedding is great,

and I have not taken a husband.

I am the midwife and she who does not bear.

I am the solace of my labour pains.

I am the bride and the bridegroom,

and it is my husband who begot me.

I am the mother of my father

and the sister of my husband

and he is my offspring.

I am the slave of him who prepared me.

I am the ruler of my offspring.

But he is the one who begot me before the time on a birthday.

And he is my offspring in (due) time,

and my power is from him.

I am the staff of his power in his youth,

and he is the rod of my old age.

And whatever he wills happens to me.

I am the silence that is incomprehensible

and the idea whose remembrance is frequent.

I am the voice whose sound is manifold

and the word whose appearance is multiple.

I am the utterance of my name.

Why, you who hate me, do you love me,

and hate those who love me?

You who deny me, confess me,

and you who confess me, deny me.

You who tell the truth about me, lie about me,

and you who have lied about me, tell the truth about me.

You who know me, be ignorant of me,

and those who have not known me, let them know me.

For I am knowledge and ignorance.

I am shame and boldness.

I am shameless; I am ashamed.

I am strength and I am fear.

I am war and peace.

Give heed to me.

I am the one who is disgraced and the great one.

Give heed to my poverty and my wealth.

Do not be arrogant to me when I am cast out upon the earth,

and you will find me in those that are to come.

And do not look upon me on the dung-heap

nor go and leave me cast out,

and you will find me in the kingdoms.

And do not look upon me when I am cast out among those who

are disgraced and in the least places,

nor laugh at me.

And do not cast me out among those who are slain in violence.

But I, I am compassionate and I am cruel.

Be on your guard!

Do not hate my obedience

and do not love my self-control.

In my weakness, do not forsake me,

and do not be afraid of my power.

For why do you despise my fear

and curse my pride?

But I am she who exists in all fears

and strength in trembling.

I am she who is weak,

and I am well in a pleasant place.

I am senseless and I am wise.

Why have you hated me in your counsels?

For I shall be silent among those who are silent,

and I shall appear and speak,

Why then have you hated me, you Greeks?

Because I am a barbarian among the barbarians?

For I am the wisdom of the Greeks

and the knowledge of the barbarians.

I am the judgement of the Greeks and of the barbarians.

I am the one whose image is great in Egypt

and the one who has no image among the barbarians.

I am the one who has been hated everywhere

and who has been loved everywhere.

I am the one whom they call Life,

and you have called Death.

I am the one whom they call Law,

and you have called Lawlessness.

I am the one whom you have pursued,

and I am the one whom you have seized.

I am the one whom you have scattered,

and you have gathered me together.

I am the one before whom you have been ashamed,

and you have been shameless to me.

I am she who does not keep festival,

and I am she whose festivals are many.

I, I am godless,

and I am the one whose God is great.

I am the one whom you have reflected upon,

and you have scorned me.

I am unlearned,

and they learn from me.

I am the one that you have despised,

and you reflect upon me.

I am the one whom you have hidden from,

and you appear to me.

But whenever you hide yourselves,

I myself will appear.

For whenever you appear,

I myself will hide from you.

Those who have [...] to it [...] senselessly [...].

Take me [... understanding] from grief.

and take me to yourselves from understanding and grief.

And take me to yourselves from places that are ugly and in ruin,

and rob from those which are good even though in ugliness.

Out of shame, take me to yourselves shamelessly;

and out of shamelessness and shame,

upbraid my members in yourselves.

And come forward to me, you who know me

and you who know my members,

and establish the great ones among the small first creatures.

Come forward to childhood,

and do not despise it because it is small and it is little.

And do not turn away greatnesses in some parts from the smallness's,

for the smallness's are known from the greatnesses.

Why do you curse me and honour me?

You have wounded and you have had mercy.

Do not separate me from the first ones whom you have known.

And do not cast anyone out nor turn anyone away

[...] turn you away and [... know] him not.

[...].

What is mine [...].

I know the first ones and those after them know me.

But I am the mind of [...] and the rest of [...].

I am the knowledge of my inquiry,

and the finding of those who seek after me,

and the command of those who ask of me,

and the power of the powers in my knowledge

of the angels, who have been sent at my word,

and of gods in their seasons by my counsel,

and of spirits of every man who exists with me,

and of women who dwell within me.

I am the one who is honoured, and who is praised,

and who is despised scornfully.

I am peace,

and war has come because of me.

And I am an alien and a citizen.

I am the substance and the one who has no substance.

Those who are without association with me are ignorant of me,

and those who are in my substance are the ones who know me.

Those who are close to me have been ignorant of me,

and those who are far away from me are the ones who have known me.

On the day when I am close to you, you are far away from me,

and on the day when I am far away from you, I am close to you.

[I am ...] within.

[I am ...] of the natures.

I am [...] of the creation of the spirits.

[...] request of the souls.

I am control and the uncontrollable.

I am the union and the dissolution.

I am the abiding and I am the dissolution.

I am the one below,

and they come up to me.

I am the judgment and the acquittal.

I, I am sinless,

and the root of sin derives from me.

I am lust in (outward) appearance,

and interior self-control exists within me.

I am the hearing which is attainable to everyone

and the speech which cannot be grasped.

I am a mute who does not speak,

and great is my multitude of words.

Hear me in gentleness, and learn of me in roughness.

I am she who cries out,

and I am cast forth upon the face of the earth.

I prepare the bread and my mind within.

I am the knowledge of my name.

I am the one who cries out,

and I listen.

I appear and [...] walk in [...] seal of my [...].

I am [...] the defense [...].

I am the one who is called Truth

and iniquity [...].

You honour me [...] and you whisper against me.

You who are vanquished, judge them (who vanquish you)

before they give judgment against you,

because the judge and partiality exist in you.

If you are condemned by this one, who will acquit you?

Or, if you are acquitted by him, who will be able to detain you?

For what is inside of you is what is outside of you,

and the one who fashions you on the outside

is the one who shaped the inside of you.

And what you see outside of you, you see inside of you;

it is visible and it is your garment.

Hear me, you hearers

and learn of my words, you who know me.

I am the hearing that is attainable to everything;

I am the speech that cannot be grasped.

I am the name of the sound

and the sound of the name.

I am the sign of the letter

and the designation of the division.

And I [...].

(3 lines missing)

[...] light [...].

[...] hearers [...] to you

[...] the great power.

And [...] will not move the name.

[...] to the one who created me.

And I will speak his name.

Look then at his words

and all the writings which have been completed.

Give heed then, you hearers

and you also, the angels and those who have been sent,

and you spirits who have arisen from the dead.

For I am the one who alone exists,

and I have no one who will judge me.

For many are the pleasant forms which exist in numerous sins,

and incontinencies,

and disgraceful passions,

and fleeting pleasures,

which (men) embrace until they become sober

and go up to their resting place.

And they will find me there,

and they will live,

and they will not die again.

Early spiritual experiences

Spirituality of one kind or another has always been important in my life. As a child living in Ardleigh, near Colchester, the town where I was born, I was brought up in the Church of England, so like most children brought up to go to church it would have been church services which gave me my first contact with spirituality.

My godmother gave me a bible, which I read with great interest, unlike many children who are given bibles by their godparents. However my parents were not greatly interested in spiritual matters. We lived on a smallholding and my father, who was born in Twinstead, worked on a fruit farm. My mother was from Stratford in London.

I was born on November 13 1953 under the sign of Scorpio, though it was only in later life that I began to take an interest in astrological matters.

As a child I always felt I was different from other children. I tended to keep myself to myself and did not find it easy to make friends with others. When I went on to secondary school I found it harder still, and had difficulty mixing with the other pupils. I did work hard though, and was successful in sciences. I enjoyed church worship and singing hymns, but lost interest after I left school.

Although I took an interest in Christianity and was interested to hear what the vicar had to tell us in church, I did not become a committed member of the Church of England and did not go to church regularly after I left school.

All my life I have been interested in photography. I took up the hobby when I was given a camera as a child, and later joined a photographic group, photographing a range of subjects including trains and cities. Images have always been important to me.

The greatest force in my life however has been my spiritual side. From my early years I felt drawn to spiritual matters. As a young adult a series of spiritual events began which changed the course of my life. They are still doing so.

Perhaps the first example was when during my schooldays I developed an interest in witchcraft. I found a book on the subject in the school library and took it home. It was called King of the Witches by June Johns, and I found it fascinating. It is considered a key book in the literature of witchcraft, because it describes in detail the rites and ceremonies of 'wicca' and their relationship to the mystic lore of past ages and knowledge of ancient secrets. However I have never tried practising witchcraft. I did light candles a few times, but did not take it any further than that.

I managed to leave school with good grades in A Level chemistry and physics, and this qualified me for a job as a laboratory assistant at ICI in Brantham. I joined the company straight from school in 1972, when I was 18. I enjoyed this work and did well at it. My employers wanted me to attend college so that I could develop my knowledge and earn promotion to a more senior post, but after the experiences I'd had at school I did not want to go back into an educational establishment. I was happy to continue in a junior post as a lab assistant.

My principal work was making polymers (long-chain organic molecules). Polymers are very important in many areas of manufacturing, particularly plastics, and are used for example in synthetic rubber, neoprene, nylon, PVC, polystyrene, polyethylene and polypropylene. I enjoyed this work and found it absorbing.

A time of darkness

In 1976, when I was 22, I had an extremely traumatic experience, although perhaps I did not realise at the time quite how disturbing it was and how far-reaching its effects would be. I came downstairs one morning to go to work to find my father lying dead on the kitchen floor. He had had a heart attack.

My father was only 62, so it was a dreadful shock both to me and my mother, who was only 53. She had to be prescribed valium after that to cope with the stress. We were close and we looked after each other. I was not very experienced in life, and I had no idea how to cope with the sudden loss of my father so unexpectedly.

After my father passed away neither of us felt we wanted to go on living in the house with all its memories, so in 1978 we left Ardleigh and moved to Chelsworth in Suffolk, where my mother took a job in an old people's home. Unfortunately the home closed two years later and we had to move into a mobile home in Ipswich. She had to manage on her widow's pension.

The death of my father was the start of a very difficult time for me. I was transferred to the research department at ICI, and things began to go seriously wrong. It was at this time that I developed psychosis, mental illness.

The most alarming symptom was that I developed an obsession with a young female laboratory assistant. I did not pester her or try to approach her - in fact she did not even know about my feelings - but I became fixated on her and could not think about anything else. I did not feel at any time that I wanted to touch her or harm her but I was always aware of where she was and what she was doing and I could not get her out of my mind.

My obsession with this woman took over completely when I was at work, and it soon became obvious to my colleagues and my boss that something was wrong. I was thinking about her all the time and watching her to see what she was doing. In my mind she was the only person that mattered. I could not concentrate on my work and my colleagues began to think I was very odd. I felt very nervous and stressed and life became quite miserable.

Something was obviously going wrong in my mind. My mother took me to see the family doctor, who examined me and asked me many questions. This was in 1978. The doctor diagnosed depression and prescribed a course of anti-depressants. When they failed to alleviate my symptoms he prescribed chlorpromazine, an antipsychotic drug which relieves the symptoms of schizophrenia. Chlorpromazine has powerful anxiety-reducing properties. Its introduction has been described as the single greatest advance in psychiatric care and has greatly improved the prognosis of patients in psychiatric hospitals.

The doctor referred me to a psychiatrist, an Indian lady, and she interviewed me at length. She was very helpful. She explained that I had suffered two great emotional shocks - the death of my father, and my obsession with the woman at work. She told me I was suffering from acute depression and said I would need to go into hospital for a few days for observation. I was admitted to Severally Mental Hospital in Colchester.

When I was admitted to hospital the chlorpromazine was stopped, and I began to suffer withdrawal symptoms. I began to feel acutely ill and very disturbed. This was a dreadful experience for me. I felt confined and threatened. At my worst I remember screaming and fighting off the staff as they were trying to inject me.

They kept me under observation and gave me more medication to reduce the effects of my illness, which was diagnosed as paranoid schizophrenia. After they gave me an injection which gave me muscle cramps, I left the hospital and ran home. The family doctor was called again and I was returned to hospital, where I was put back on chlorpromazine.

I felt extremely threatened and my condition grew worse. I began to hallucinate and suffered delusions about trains. The hospital seemed to me a terrifying maze from which I could never escape. At one point my condition became so serious that I had to be sectioned, and was not able to leave the hospital. I had to spend about three weeks in the hospital while they stabilised my condition.

Severalls Mental Hospital has since been closed because modern, more enlightened approaches have since been adopted for the treatment of people with mental illness.

Eventually my condition stabilised enough for me to be discharged. Later in 1978 I went back to work and found I could cope well as long as I had regular medication. I have been on medication ever since, except for a period which I will talk about later in this book.

An introduction to the
Unification Church

One day in 1980 while I was in Ipswich I met a woman from the Unification Church, the religious movement founded by the Korean religious leader Sun Myung Moon. I liked this woman and was drawn into conversation with her. She invited me to attend services with her and her friends and fellow-worshippers in Swindon. I was interested in them as people as well as in what they had to say on spiritual matters.

I knew nothing about the Unification Church at the time but I soon learned about the church and its background. It was formally established in Seoul, South Korea, as The Holy Spirit Association for the Unification of World Christianity. In 1994, it was renamed the Family Federation for World Peace and Unification.

The Unification Church attracted members from all over the world and its membership was estimated to be as many as several million people. The church and its members were involved in political, cultural, commercial, media, educational and other activities. In the English-speaking world members are usually known by non-members as 'Moonies' after the name of Sun Myung Moon.

Unification Church beliefs are summarized in the textbook Divine Principle and include belief in a universal God, striving toward the creation of a literal Kingdom of God on earth, and the universal salvation of all people, good and evil, living and dead. Sun Myung Moon is seen as their Messiah.

Getting involved with two different forms of Christianity made me start thinking about religion and what it all meant, and about the connections between the different forms of spirituality.

However, in the early 1980s, I started to have my doubts about the Unification Church. The Moonies had become a controversial organisation which had drawn a great deal of criticism for some of its policies, such as supporting the US President Richard Nixon at the time of his impeachment over the Watergate affair and arguing for a world government which would unite church and state. Sun Myung Moon was convicted of tax fraud and sent to jail.

Media in the USA and UK reported on the high-pressure recruitment methods the church used and alleged that it separated vulnerable young people from their families through the use of brainwashing and mind control. The British Government spent four years investigating the Moonies, although no charges were brought. The Daily Mail newspaper brought a case against the church, exposing the methods by which they attracted young recruits and kept them separated from their families. The newspaper won an important legal victory and the court agreed that the Mail was right to condemn the Unification Church as "the church that breaks up families". I felt I could no longer support the church, so I decided to withdraw from it and to think about other spiritual directions.

Around this time I went to London and was invited to join Hare Krishna, the Hindu religious movement founded in 1966. This was another non-sectarian religious movement, but I did not feel it offered the spiritual enlightenment I was seeking.

I also spoke to people representing the Church of Scientology, the controversial religion founded by L Ron Hubbard in 1952. But scientoloogy did not appeal to me.

The blue ovals and ancient Egypt

I now felt my spiritual interest being drawn in a new direction. After I left the Unification Church I read a book called Initiation, by Elizabeth Haich, a spiritual teacher and the author of several books on spirituality. She claimed in the book that in a past life she had been a pupil of Ptahhotep, an ancient Egyptian official who is considered to have been one of the first philosophers.

It was after reading Initiation that I began to have visions of patterns of electric blue oval shapes. I was very puzzled by this at first, but I learned that the blue oval is a symbol of the feminine transformative powers. I felt these visions were calling me to carry out spiritual work for the Goddess. I had been interested in ancient Egypt before, but these visions of blue ovals made me take a deeper interest and I began reading books about it.

I attended a talk by a spiritual person about ancient Egypt and felt I needed to learn more about it. After I became interested in ancient Egypt I decided to join the Fellowship of Isis, an international spiritual organization devoted to promoting awareness of the Goddess Isis. The Fellowship sees the Goddess Isis as the Deity.

The Fellowship had then only recently been founded, in 1976. The founders believed Isis best represented the energies of the dawning Aquarian Age, as the sun at the vernal equinox moves from the constellation of Pisces into Aquarius, because of the precession of the Earth's axis. The Fellowship is a multi-faith, multi-racial, and multi-cultural organization which dedicated to honouring the religion of all the Goddesses and pantheons throughout the planet. It welcomes people belonging to established religions as well as pagans. It now has more than 21,000 members and there are no vows of secrecy and no restrictions on joining or leaving. It is organized on a democratic basis and all members have equal privileges within it and membership is free.

In 1988 I became very ill once again. This happened because I thought my doctor had told me that he wanted to reduce my medication, so I stopped taking it (later he told me that this had not been his intention). It was a serious mistake, because my illness immediately came back. I began hearing voices and became very disturbed once again. I could no longer cope with my work, so I resigned from my job at ICI and have not been able to work since. I had to go back into hospital.

It was after my medication was stopped in 1988 that my supernatural experiences began. I felt that I had received a visitation in my home and that I was being noticed by someone and they wanted me to know this. I was aware of a presence and thought I was destined never to have sex. But I had to go back to hospital and be put on medication until 1997. In 1997 my Doctor said I was well enough not to need medication.

The Goddess Quan Yin

The first Mind Body Spirit Festival took place at the Olympia Exhibition Centre in London in 1977. It became an annual event which continues to this day, and 20 years later, in 1997, I attended the event in Manchester while I was on holiday there. I found it very interesting. I went to Mind Body Spirit several times after that.

Mind Body Spirit was about the relationship between religion, the paranormal, spirituality, natural healing, consciousness and personal growth with the aim of making these ideas more accessible to everyone. It dealt with many issues that were important to me and I took a great interest in much of what I was able to learn there, particularly in Tarot readings.

Mind Body Spirit went on to be presented in New York, Los Angeles, Cork, San Francisco, Sydney, Melbourne and in many other major cities, with leading authors and authorities giving lectures and workshops as well as a mix of new age music and performances. It is still going on as an annual event in London and Manchester. Exhibitors include the Hare Krishna devotees, the Aetherius Society, Christian groups, Buddhist groups, astrologers, Tarot readers, vegetarians, vegans, Tai Chi groups, the Anthroposophical Society, Reiki and many other New Age groups.

While at the Mind Body Spirit event in Manchester in 1997 I underwent a fascinating and revealing experience. I encountered a lady called Suma Ching Hai, who I learned practised a method of meditation advocated by the Goddess Quan Yin.

11

In Buddhism Quan Yin is associated with compassion, as venerated by East Asian Buddhists, usually as a female. The name is derived from 'Guanshiyin', which means "Observing the Sounds (or Cries) of the World". Some Buddhists believe that when one of their adherents departs from this world, they are placed by Quan Yin in the heart of a lotus, then sent home to the pure land of Sukhavati. Quan Yin is known in English as the Mercy Goddess and is revered by Chinese Taoists as an immortal.

I learned that Suma Ching Hai had founded the Immeasurable Light Meditation Centre and the Way of Sound Contemplation. She describes the Quan Yin method as "the way of the universe, a universal law that we must follow if we want to get back to the Origin, back to our true Self, back to the Kingdom of God or our Buddha nature." I bought her book, The Key of Immediate Enlightenment, and found it very enlightening. I am still studying it.

After the encounter I experienced what appeared to be an initiation with Quan Ying in my home.

Suma Ching Hai initiates spiritual aspirants into the Quan Yin method, which is purported to exist in various religions under different names, as the best way to achieve enlightenment. The method involves meditation on the "inner light and the inner sound of God", or the Shabd which she claims is also referred to in the Bible and said to be acknowledged repeatedly in the literature of all the world's major spiritual traditions. The Quan Yin method is open to people from all backgrounds and religious affiliations – you don't have to change your present religion or belief.

Encounters with the Goddess Virgo and 'They'

After this period I began to have some remarkable experiences connected to the Goddess Virgo. At the time I wanted to record these in a diary, but was advised not to by spiritual communication as it was thought that it might confuse people if the diary was read. The following account of these experiences may not be entirely accurate, as I am writing the account some years later.

Virgo's weakness in the psychic realm is to over-use her power in trying to cure the ills of the world and become emotionally and spiritually fatigued. I realised that I was seeing her because she was descending to Earth to rest.

A mysterious image of Virgo

This picture reminds me of the dark side of Virgo

This painting of Virgo as a sign of the Zodiac
reminds me of the occultist I met

An image of Virgo as pure and celestial

Virgo, Queen of Heaven

Virgo: The Virgin Goddess

A being of pure, innocent, lightness of spirit
The Virgin Goddess looks serenely out upon
The darkness that threatens to pervade her realm.
She reveals purity in never hiding her bareness.
Indeed she is so innocent, she does not know
the darkside, for she has never
walked anywhere but in the light.
She is beauty and symmetry and everything
in this world that is light and true.

– Sun Spirit Gallery

The Goddess Virgo turned out to be a merger between a spiritual person of an alien race and Virgo, a human being who lived on Earth thousands of years ago.

The Goddess Virgo as she appeared to me was in the form of a spirit body. I encountered a number of alien spirits during the course of my spiritual work, but the first memory of spiritual communication was the sound of a snigger in the distance and I inferred this to be either Isis or Virgo.

The Goddess Virgo first asked me to go to my bedroom, where a discourse would take place. Several times this occurred, and during the course of these conversations I was put in touch with the Manningtree Circle and an Egyptian occult group of the Left Hand Path from London. These groups may have been imaginary, but my experience of them was to put me in good stead when the Goddess put me in touch with firstly the spiritual form of the community known as 'They' and then a human community of They people.

This began when I felt myself summoned upstairs by a spiritual entity who belonged to 'They'. I could not describe this presence, but it was a frightening experience. I felt They were alien beings, the entities which some know as ghosts. They were cold, intellectual beings, and not pleasant to deal with. I could not see them clearly - they appeared as faint, ghostly images. I felt They were studying me and challenging me.

The alien spirits known as They were frightening to encounter. They were depressed intellectual spirits who questioned me continually as to the nature of Isis, and this communication was accompanied by the appearance of a visible white psychic material. After the encounter with They I was told that if I could survive them I could survive anything. After these encounters the Goddess Virgo put me in touch with the Spiritual Kingdom from the USA.

I remember once seeing the Goddess come down into my body to rest. I also remember the Goddess descending into my bedroom to view my laptop computer, which was a novelty then. I saw the Goddess walking down my road "leading me away", as it was put, which was a polite way of saying I was being led to my death, although this threat never came to anything.

The Goddess travelled from east to west in my living room, and I realised that even the cat from next door had become aware of her presence. The Goddess had long black hair and rosy cheeks and wore a light blue cloak and boots. Apart from watching over the UK and USA, the Goddess had been to Australia and in Her make-up was an Australian Spirit.

During this time I also became aware of She. The Goddess Virgo asked me while I was in a Bangladeshi restaurant what the Indian equivalent of Sekhmet was and I replied "Kali". It was then that She came into my soul. This She was a different She that gives decrees through Her world, a spirituality from our own spiritual realms. I called her She of Ishtar as Ishtar gave me her spirituality complex to me A spiritual thread was cut, giving me a bout of pins and needles which I thought I would die from. I also had to deal with an occultist who considered herself immortal and described herself as a Christian/pagan. She wanted to travel the universe after she had passed over. Her spirit body entered heaven and she caused mayhem for a while. Some part of her may be in heaven now, but I had to deal with her spirit and had many days when I thought I was in communication with her.

She put her spiritual coffin in my loft and eventually withdrew. She was part of a group of three occult women with a group soul.

After the Goddess Virgo had put me in touch with these groups I was handed over to God in the form of the 'Above', which is heaven as I understand it. I came to understand that there was a heavenly collapse and saw a number of spirits tearing at their chests as though they were of Jewish origin.

Encounters with Her, the Beast and Spirits

Apart from the Goddess Virgo I became aware of another alien spirit of the same race as that of the Goddess Virgo. This race of people all shared the name of Her. This particular spirit gave me a lot of spiritual work to do, dealing with all sorts of demons and alien spirits while overseeing the Her in the Goddess Virgo. Other Her world spirits included one that accompanied me on a trip to Brussels dressed in red and black and I often saw this one looking in my living room and putting lilac psychic material around the ceiling.

During the time I was in contact with the Goddess Virgo I was also visited by another Her Being, the Being known in the Bible as the Beast. Revelation Chapter 17 verse 8: "The beast that you saw was and is not and will ascend out of the bottomless pit and go to perdition."

I was also contacted by an occultist in London who was working to release the the Her being, called a Beast in the Book of Revelation, from a pit in which it was trapped. The knowledge came to me that she had succeeded.

While in Brussels I saw another Her world spirit sitting at a desk dressed in green and black. This one said something which made me angry and a Babylonian knife came from off my shoulder and landed on the desk, a threat on my part which in turn made this Her angry. Eventually the Her spirit in the Goddess became detached from Virgo and when that happened Virgo thanked me.

Virgo then disappeared in the form of a black "verve" and went out of existence. The Her spirit from the Goddess Virgo remains with me to this day, together with a spirit body.

I also became aware of a spirit I called "Mattin". This spirit was very friendly and intellectual. Her called it "Her mind" and wanted to be put in a dark basement. Other spirits I came across were called Bibes and Kriels. Bibes were sweet little spirits which liked being put in wooden pots and placed in woodland. Kriels were not so nice and were very aggressive, and looked for hard-headed people to enter. I also saw a sprite, which left my house in a shaft of gold screaming "Become a Christian child, Peter Howe, become a Christian child" and went in the direction of my neighbour's house.

I am sure my neighbour got caught up in this activity, but whether she was aware of it I have no idea. The Her spirit had to gather all her psychic material from the USA and got entangled in a pub and my neighbour's house. This psychic material condensed in me as dots. But the Her spirit was concerned for the neighbour's children and did a lot of spiritual work to ensure their spiritual well being.

I also had the impression that I was being put in touch with a government reality department, and had contact with a spiritual race known to me as Americans who were Satanic. They called themselves the Government and travelled like blobs of gold.

I also came across a spiritual Her World Being which had long blonde hair. As far as I know it engaged in spiritual battle in Europe and won. So that makes five I came across between 1997 and 2003.

One episode when dealing with the Goddess Virgo was when I was sitting on a bench outside. Virgo tried to help me overcome my shyness with women but was stopped by They as they didn't want Virgo to give spiritual instructions down here.

Her Beings, Devils and Demons

Around this time I had a vision of the Her being, called a Beast in the Book of Revelation, that was released from the pit. It appeared flying along the railway line into Manningtree station. It was clutching an embryo to its body and I felt it was going to leave it somewhere in the area.

On a holiday to Amsterdam the same Her being, in the shape of a woman, sat beside me on Waterloo Station and got on the train to Brussels.

Another very vivid vision I have seen was of a figure I call the 'Pirate' because his clothes look like those of a pirate. I also see him as one of the Four Horsemen of the Apocalypse. He is linked to this Her Being by the tricorn hat it wears.

During a holiday in Harwich I was also visited by green and black salamander demons that attack the Christian realm.

One day I was aggressively chased by a youth. I did not feel scared and ordered him away. I pointed a finger at him and cried "Out!" and heard a crack. I saw him again a while later and saw that he was calm and no longer hostile.

I also came across a spiritual Her World being who had long blonde hair. I believe this being engaged in a victorious spiritual battle in Europe.

I saw a vision of a ring of a complex design, and I decided to look for one to match the vision. I found a similar ring in a local jewellers and I now always wear it.

My mother never seemed to be aware of my visions, but she was very supportive of my problems. But during the period from 1997 to 2003 my paranoid schizophrenia was getting the better of me. I had another very traumatic life event in 2003 when my mother died, at the age of 80, as suddenly as my father. She came home from the shops and had a seizure. She was taken to hospital, where she died. This was the start of another very difficult period for me.

One day later that year I walked up to Lawford Churchyard and was sitting there when a police officer approached me. Unfortunately I assaulted him, scratching his face, though I could not say exactly why I did this except that I was very unwell at the time. This event led to a court hearing and I was sectioned. I spent six months in acute ward, followed by a year under observation in a day ward. This was much less stressful than the first time.

My spiritual experiences have been reflected in other aspects of my life. I greatly admire the long-established rock band Jethro Tull and their lead singer and flute player Ian Anderson, whom I know to be a very spiritual man. I have been following them for many years. My favourite Jethro Tull album is Thick As A Brick (1972), their early concept album consisting of a single very long track.

Postscript – further experiences

My most recent spiritual experience happened in February 2011. The spiritual being Her returned and told me It was merging with me. Before long the Being named Her went out of existence, but before this happened we had to work with the other Beings to help them to expire. It was when She was in Her mind that it was decreed that Her world was incompatible with Earth, because after communication from me, Her people put She in their minds. She is from a different place.

First the Her Being of Revelation Chapter 17 in the painting that I named the Devil went to the USA after depositing the woman who was with it. There was conversation between this Devil and the Her in green and black, and both went out of existence. The one with blonde hair tried to become a permanent fixture in London but I helped to remove it and it died at the hands of a swordsman, pictured in the third painting. Also during this time a Her world entity that called a Below person had to be dealt with, which makes six in total that I came across at this time, but there were three others attached to Her Majesty's Government. One was named the God Her and another attached to universalists and shut out by the Government and was at loggerheads with the Occult Her which was attached to Government buildings. There was a Her mind attached to Palace buildings.

Her and the Government

All these beings came from Her world, but there was a reason for this - an occultist Her being came to this country and attached itself to the Government. This Her Being was not meant to come here, but should have gone to another planet. Its mind also reached the USA. It came here I believe during the reign of Elizabeth I, due to an occult event which no one is sure about. It came here to protect Christianity.

Also attached to the Government was another Her being. It was against the presence of the occult Her because it was not meant to be here, but the task of this Her was antagonise the Government because the Government had become influential over the occult and spiritual lives of the country. It had become shut out and caused a reality problem when the occult Her had gone. The schism in splitting the occult people from spiritual people, ie religious people, was due to the presence, I believe, of the occult Her, which was not meant to be here.

This splitting of the occult world from Christianity has to be resolved by dialogue now, together with the acceptance by Christianity of the occult nature of its religion.

Also around this time a They entity called a Fairy was removed from Manningtree. That evening Darkness arrived to help remove the Swordsman from London, together with a Salamander element, otherwise known as Harwich.

The next day I went to London by train and during that day the Her entity that was in my head came and went out of existence. This entity then discovered another They entity in London and this, together with a They being that was with me, stayed in London.

On Sunday, one of the entities I call They went away because of universal problems. The following Monday a conversation took place with London people which included a Christian, and the other They being died. A group of people who have Her world characteristics are now dealing with their problems.

Conclusions for Christianity

The experiences that have been related here have consequences for understanding Christian scriptures. When one looks at the first verses of the Book of Genesis, God creates Heaven and Earth and in the following verses it is apparent that others termed 'Us' as well as the Lord God did the creating. I have come to understand that the Lord God came from the world of She, and this is backed up by Gnostic literature.

I believe that Satan came here at the same time, but from a different place. Satan came from two worlds, the worlds of He and Her. Satan was a Being who was a conglomerate of He and Her minds.

The books of the Old Testament tell of the relationship between the Lord God and the Jews, while the New Testament tells the story of Jesus. In the Gospel of Luke it is clear to me that the conception of Mary's child was of the Holy Spirit, but that she was overshadowed by the God of the Most High. Therefore, in order for Jesus to be called the Son of God, it seems to me that the Father gave his only begotten Son to be born in Mary's child. Because I have witnessed one of Her Beings putting its offspring into someone, I believe the Father did the same thing with His offspring by putting Him into Mary's child. Therefore I do not believe it is necessary to introduce the concept of the virgin birth.

I believe the Gospels make it clear when Jesus talks of the Son and of the Father that the Son is of the Father and part of Jesus. I believe that because the only begotten Son of the Father was part of Jesus this explains the occult nature of the resurrection and ascension. This event was unique because of this.

In the Book of Revelation it seems clear to me that the Father and the Son are from the world of He and are not related to the Lord God.

In Revelation Chapter 12 the woman I knew as Virgo was being pursued by Satan (a He-Her constructed mind).

Book of Revelation, Chapter 12

1   And there appeared a great wonder in heaven; a woman clothed with the sun, and the moon under her feet, and upon her head a crown of twelve stars:

2   And she being with child cried, travailing in birth, and pained to be delivered.

3   And there appeared another wonder in heaven; and behold a great red dragon, having seven heads and ten horns, and seven crowns upon his heads.

4   And his tail drew the third part of the stars of heaven, and did cast them to the earth: and the dragon stood before the woman which was ready to be delivered, for to devour her child as soon as it was born.

5   And she brought forth a man child, who was to rule all nations with a rod of iron: and her child was caught up unto God, and to his throne.

6   And the woman fled into the wilderness, where she hath a place prepared of God, that they should feed her there a thousand two hundred and threescore days.

7   And there was war in heaven: Michael and his angels fought against the dragon; and the dragon fought and his angels,

8   And prevailed not; neither was their place found any more in heaven.

9   And the great dragon was cast out, that old serpent, called the Devil, and Satan, which deceiveth the whole world: he was cast out into the earth, and his angels were cast out with him.

10 And I heard a loud voice saying in heaven, Now is come salvation, and strength, and the kingdom of our God, and the power of his Christ: for the accuser of our brethren is cast down, which accused them before our God day and night.

11 And they overcame him by the blood of the Lamb, and by the word of their testimony; and they loved not their lives unto the death.

12 Therefore rejoice, ye heavens, and ye that dwell in them. Woe to the inhabiters of the earth and of the sea! for the devil is come down unto you, having great wrath, because he knoweth that he hath but a short time.

13 And when the dragon saw that he was cast unto the earth, he persecuted the woman which brought forth the man child.

14 And to the woman were given two wings of a great eagle, that she might fly into the wilderness, into her place, where she is nourished for a time, and times, and half a time, from the face of the serpent.

15 And the serpent cast out of his mouth water as a flood after the woman, that he might cause her to be carried away of the flood.

16 And the earth helped the woman, and the earth opened her mouth, and swallowed up the flood which the dragon cast out of his mouth.

17 And the dragon was wroth with the woman, and went to make war with the remnant of her seed, which keep the commandments of God, and have the testimony of Jesus Christ.

Book of Revelation, Chapter 13

In Revelation Chapter 13 the Her Being here known as Beast is given authority by Satan, and I believe it to be the Her Being that was with Virgo.

1   And I stood upon the sand of the sea, and saw a beast rise up out of the sea, having seven heads and ten horns, and upon his horns ten crowns, and upon his heads the name of blasphemy.

2   And the beast which I saw was like unto a leopard, and his feet were as the feet of a bear, and his mouth as the mouth of a lion: and the dragon gave him his power, and his seat, and great authority.

3   And I saw one of his heads as it were wounded to death; and his deadly wound was healed: and all the world wondered after the beast.

4   And they worshipped the dragon which gave power unto the beast: and they worshipped the beast, saying, Who is like unto the beast? who is able to make war with him?

5   And there was given unto him a mouth speaking great things and blasphemies; and power was given unto him to continue forty and two months.

6   And he opened his mouth in blasphemy against God, to blaspheme his name, and his tabernacle, and them that dwell in heaven.

7   And it was given unto him to make war with the saints, and to overcome them: and power was given him over all kindreds, and tongues, and nations.

8   And all that dwell upon the earth shall worship him, whose names are not written in the book of life of the Lamb slain from the foundation of the world.

9   If any man have an ear, let him hear.

10   He that leadeth into captivity shall go into captivity: he that killeth with the sword must be killed with the sword. Here is the patience and the faith of the saints.

11   And I beheld another beast coming up out of the earth; and he had two horns like a lamb, and he spake as a dragon.

12   And he exerciseth all the power of the first beast before him, and causeth the earth and them which dwell therein to worship the first beast, whose deadly wound was healed.

13   And he doeth great wonders, so that he maketh fire come down from heaven on the earth in the sight of men,

14   And deceiveth them that dwell on the earth by the means of those miracles which he had power to do in the sight of the beast; saying to them that dwell on the earth, that they should make an image to the beast, which had the wound by a sword, and did live.

15   And he had power to give life unto the image of the beast, that the image of the beast should both speak, and cause that as many as would not worship the image of the beast should be killed.

16 And he causeth all, both small and great, rich and poor, free and bond, to receive a mark in their right hand, or in their foreheads:

17 And that no man might buy or sell, save he that had the mark, or the name of the beast, or the number of his name.

18 Here is wisdom. Let him that hath understanding count the number of the beast: for it is the number of a man; and his number is Six hundred threescore and six.

Book of Revelation, Chapter 17

In Chapter 17 the Her Being called a Beast is the one that was released from the bottomless pit by the occultist.

1   And there came one of the seven angels which had the seven vials, and talked with me, saying unto me, Come hither; I will shew unto thee the judgment of the great whore that sitteth upon many waters:

2   With whom the kings of the earth have committed fornication, and the inhabitants of the earth have been made drunk with the wine of her fornication.

3   So he carried me away in the spirit into the wilderness: and I saw a woman sit upon a scarlet coloured beast, full of names of blasphemy, having seven heads and ten horns.

4   And the woman was arrayed in purple and scarlet colour, and decked with gold and precious stones and pearls, having a golden cup in her hand full of abominations and filthiness of her fornication:

5   And upon her forehead was a name written, MYSTERY, BABYLON THE GREAT, THE MOTHER OF HARLOTS AND ABOMINATIONS OF THE EARTH.

6   And I saw the woman drunken with the blood of the saints, and with the blood of the martyrs of Jesus: and when I saw her, I wondered with great admiration.

7   And the angel said unto me, Wherefore didst thou marvel? I will tell thee the mystery of the woman, and of the beast that carrieth her, which hath the seven heads and ten horns.

8   The beast that thou sawest was, and is not; and shall ascend out of the bottomless pit, and go into perdition: and they that dwell on the earth shall wonder, whose names were not written in the book of life from the foundation of the world, when they behold the beast that was, and is not, and yet is.

9   And here is the mind which hath wisdom. The seven heads are seven mountains, on which the woman sitteth.

10   And there are seven kings: five are fallen, and one is, and the other is not yet come; and when he cometh, he must continue a short space.

11   And the beast that was, and is not, even he is the eighth, and is of the seven, and goeth into perdition.

12   And the ten horns which thou sawest are ten kings, which have received no kingdom as yet; but receive power as kings one hour with the beast.

13   These have one mind, and shall give their power and strength unto the beast.

14   These shall make war with the Lamb, and the Lamb shall overcome them: for he is Lord of lords, and King of kings: and they that are with him are called, and chosen, and faithful.

15 And he saith unto me, The waters which thou sawest, where the whore sitteth, are peoples, and multitudes, and nations, and tongues.

16 And the ten horns which thou sawest upon the beast, these shall hate the whore, and shall make her desolate and naked, and shall eat her flesh, and burn her with fire.

17 For God hath put in their hearts to fulfil his will, and to agree, and give their kingdom unto the beast, until the words of God shall be fulfilled.

18 And the woman which thou sawest is that great city, which reigneth over the kings of the earth.

The end

This concludes my work for the Goddess.

Satistar

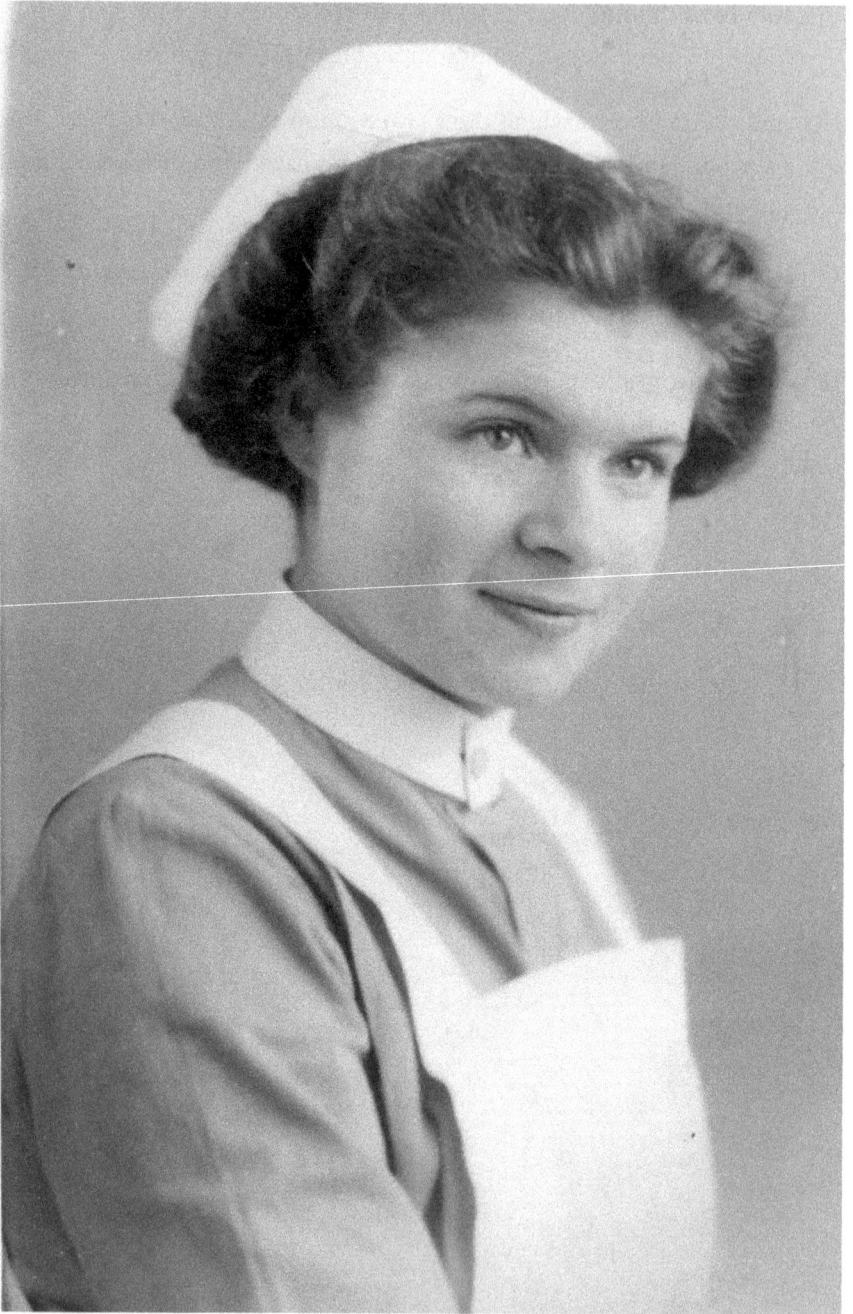
My Mother

My Mother

This shows the Her being I saw flying into the station

Virgo as I saw her when she visited my home

I see this figure as a pirate or time lord

www.ingramcontent.com/pod-product-compliance
Lightning Source LLC
Chambersburg PA
CBHW061514040426
42450CB00008B/1616